PRAYING
with the
SAINTS
Prayers for the Sick and Dying

PRAYING
with the
SAINTS
Prayers for the Sick and Dying

Wyatt North
BOOKS THAT INSPIRE

CONTENTS

ABOUT WYATT NORTH

Starting out with just one writer in 2012, Wyatt North Publishing has expanded to include writers from across the country. Our writers include college professors, theologians, and historians. Wyatt North is a trusted source for Catholic readers looking for inspirational books. Visit WyattNorth.com to sign up for free books and promotions, and to view our catalog.

INTRODUCTION

There are few guarantees in life. Nonetheless, for all of us, who are born in the flesh, it is a sure thing that we will all experience sickness and eventually death. The prospect of one's mortality can be intimidating—the experience of loss, when those whom we love die, can cause immense pain and sorrow. For Christians, however, we have an answer to these problems that allows us to persist through sickness and death in hope.

This booklet may be used for those who are sick or nearing death. It may also encourage those struck with fear over a loved one's illness or impending passing. All of the saints, whose meditations we reflect upon, have died even as we will. Let us take comfort, then, from these meditations. More than that, might these testimonies of faith grant us confidence, courage, and endurance to face sickness and death with hope.

A MEDITATION FROM ST. CATHERINE OF SIENNA

One of the most common themes in the writings of the saints concerning death and dying is how God draws us closer to Him through sickness, pain, suffering, and even mourning. Saint Catherine of Sienna, like many medieval persons, suffered from a variety of ailments. During the last year of her life, she was unable to eat and lost the use of her legs. Yet, she recognized in such sorrow how to approach her ailments with patience, courage, and faith.

A Meditation from St. Catherine of Sienna

Very pleasing to Me, dearest daughter, is the willing desire to bear every pain and fatigue, even unto death, for the salvation of souls, for the more the soul endures, the more she shows that she loves Me; loving Me she comes to know more of My truth, and the more she knows, the more pain and intolerable grief she feels at the offenses committed against Me. You asked Me to sustain you, and to punish the faults of others in you, and you did not remark that you were really asking for love, light, and knowledge of the truth, since I have already told you that, by the increase of love, grows grief and pain, wherefore he that grows in love grows in grief. Therefore, I say to you all, that you should ask, and it will be given you, for I deny nothing to him who asks of Me in truth. Consider that the love of divine charity is so closely joined in the soul with perfect patience, that neither can leave the soul without the other. For this reason (if the soul elect to love Me) she should elect to endure pains for Me in whatever mode or circumstance I may send them to her. Patience cannot be proved in any other way than by suffering, and patience is united with love as has been said. Therefore bear yourselves with manly courage, for, unless you do so, you will not prove yourselves to be spouses of My Truth, and faithful children, nor of the company of those who relish the taste of My honor, and the salvation of souls.

A Treatise of Divine
Providence

Additional Biblical Reflections: Psalm 37:7–9; Luke 8:15; Romans 12:12 ; 2 Peter 3:9.

Prayer

Lord, in great patience, you endure our faithlessness so that we might be preserved until life in your name. Grant us patience as we endure sorrow in the world. Let us ever be mindful that through patient suffering, we learn to rely on you more. As I/[NAME] endure(s) this present ailment, grant me/him/her the same. In Jesus' name. Amen.

A MEDITATION FROM ST. BERNARD

One of the gravest spiritual challenges, when we are ailing or even dying, is that we can no longer attend Mass with the faithful. This is where we have grown accustomed to hearing the Gospel, receiving the Blessed Sacrament, and meditating on God's holy truths. It is likewise where we've found consolation amongst other believers during life's various trials. Thus, it may seem, if we are bound to a bed or hospital, that our bodies have prevented us from loving God in the ways we've learned to do. Likewise, if loving one's neighbor is the way that Christ commanded us to love Him and the Father, if we are unable to perform acts of charity, how can we draw nearer to God's love ourselves? Still, in our sufferings, we might find a new intimacy with the one who took on fresh, frail like ours, and suffered even as we do. For it is in suffering and sorrow that Christ was glorified most highly.

A Meditation from St. Bernard

In this life, I think, we cannot fully and perfectly obey that precept, 'Thou shalt love the Lord thy God with all thy heart, and with all thy soul, and with all thy strength, and with all thy mind' (Luke 10.27). For here the heart must take thought for the body; and the soul must energize the flesh; and the strength must guard itself from impairment. And by God's favor, must seek to increase. It is therefore impossible to offer up all our being to

God, to yearn altogether for His face, so long as we must accommodate our purposes and aspirations to these fragile, sickly bodies of ours. Wherefore the soul may hope to possess the fourth degree of love, or rather to be possessed by it, only when it has been clothed upon with that spiritual and immortal body, which will be perfect, peaceful, lovely, and in everything wholly subjected to the spirit. And to this degree no human effort can attain: it is in God's power to give it to whom He wills. Then the soul will easily reach that highest stage, because no lusts of the flesh will retard its eager entrance into the joy of its Lord, and no troubles will disturb its peace. May we not think that the holy martyrs enjoyed this grace, in some degree at least, before they laid down their victorious bodies? Surely that was immeasurable strength of love which enraptured their souls, enabling them to laugh at fleshly torments and to yield their lives gladly. But even though the frightful pain could not destroy their peace of mind, it must have impaired somewhat its perfection.

St. Bernard of
Clairvaux. *On Loving
God*, Ch 10

Additional Biblical Reflections: Leviticus 19:18; Matthew 22:1–46; Luke 10:27.

Prayer

Lord, how can we love you with all our soul, body, and mind when our bodies and even our minds falter? By uniting ourselves to you, and your suffering, our broken bodies join you in brokenness. Should we fall ill, or even die, grant us full assurance so that we might follow you likewise into life everlasting and the fullest embrace of your love. Amen.

A MEDITATION FROM ST. FRANCIS OF ASSISI

I n his monastic rule, Saint Francis regularly exhorted his fellow monks to live in scarcity and solitude. However, the one exception to this was when a brother was sick, or one was nearing death. In such instances, he recommended that all material comforts be given to the ailing, and all company should be kept. For in such moments, we draw closer to our Lord's spirit of compassion than we do when under normal circumstances as scarcity prevents us from the trappings of materialism. This is because it is in communion with the Body of Christ, where all things are shared, and we care for one another, that we come to encounter Christ most intimately.

A Meditation from St. Francis of Assisi

If any of the brothers fall into sickness, wherever he may be, let the others not leave him, unless one of the brothers, or more if it be necessary, be appointed to serve him as they would wish to be served themselves; but in urgent necessity they may commit him to some person who will take care of him in his infirmity. And I ask the sick brother that he give thanks to the Creator for all things, and that he desire to be as God wills him to be, whether sick or well; for all whom the Lord has predestined to eternal life are disciplined by the rod of afflictions and infirmities, and the spirit of compunction; as the Lord says: "Such as I love I rebuke and chastise."

If, however, he be disquieted and angry, either against God or against the brothers, or perhaps ask eagerly for remedies, desiring too much to deliver his body which is soon to die, which is an enemy to the soul, this comes to him from evil and he is fleshly, and seems not to be of the brothers, because he loves his body more than his soul.

St. Francis of Assisi,
First Rule of the Friars
Minor

Additional Biblical Reflections: Ecclesiastes 4:9–12; Hebrews 10:24–25; Romans 12:3–33.

Prayer

Lord, there is no treasure in this world greater in value than the love of one another. There is no treasure greater even more than the treasures stored up for us in the Kingdom of Heaven. Whether we are ailing ourselves or petitioning on behalf of the ill, let us embrace the treasure of one another, for the one thing that persists beyond this life is the communion of the saints. Let us take solace in the fact that those whom we console or are consoled by will remain one with us, in Christ, even if death should separate us. Amen.

A MEDITATION FROM ST. THERESE OF LISIEUX

S aint Therese of Lisieux died at only twenty-four years of age. She endured many bodily ailments. Nonetheless, through her sickness and frailty, she found intimacy with God and her fellow sisters. Even in her trials, she saw God glorified in her suffering. It is not uncommon, nor is it sinful, to experience fear in death. Even Jesus sweated beads of blood when he knew his suffering and death approached. However, a godly fear drives us not toward anger but gratitude. Let us recognize, when death befalls us or those whom we love, thanksgiving for the many blessings God has bestowed upon us in life and the greater blessings that still await us.

A Meditation from St. Therese of Lisieux

One evening I was alone with my uncle, and he talked so tenderly of my Mother and of bygone days that I was deeply moved and began to cry. My sensitiveness touched him too; he was surprised that one of my age should feel as I did. So he determined to do all he could to divert my mind during the holidays. But God had decided otherwise. That very evening my headache became acute, and I was seized with a strange shivering which lasted all night. My aunt, like a real mother, never left me for a moment; all through my illness she lavished on me the most tender and devoted care. You may imagine my poor Father's grief when he returned from Paris to find me in this hopeless state; he thought I was going to die, but Our Lord might have said to him: "This sickness is not unto death, but for the glory of God." Yes, God was glorified by means of this trial, by the wonderful resignation of my Father and sisters. And to Marie especially what suffering it brought, and how grateful I am to this dear sister! She seemed to divine my wants by instinct, for a mother's heart is more knowing than the science of the most skillful doctors.

St. Therese, *The Story of
the Springtime of a Little
White Flower*

Additional Biblical Reflections: Psalm 73:26; Matthew 5:1–3; John 11:4.

Prayer

Dearest Lord, you are glorified in all things. Grant us faith to see the treasures in Heaven we have yet to receive so that we might persist in gratitude no matter what befalls us. Grant us the consolation of family and friends, and may we be such consolation to others. In Jesus' name. Amen.

A MEDITATION FROM
ST. BERNARD

W̶e care for our bodies, even as we near death or we ail, not
merely because comforting the body relieves our suffering
but because our bodies are good. God did not declare the
first man and woman "good" until after he breathed life into human
nostrils. He, similarly, did not leave Christ in the grave to raise him as
a mere spirit but brought him back as the perfect man, in body and
soul. Likewise, while we who are apart from the body when we die are
surely with the Lord, we believe in the resurrection. However, while
these bodies suffer and hurt, the bodies in the resurrection will know
no suffering, pain, or death. Thus, let us look forward to the day when
our glorified bodies will be fully united to Christ in his glory.

A Meditation from St. Bernard

*What of the souls already released from their bodies? We believe that
they are overwhelmed in that vast sea of eternal light and of luminous
eternity. But no one denies that they still hope and desire to receive their
bodies again: whence it is plain that they are not yet wholly transformed,
and that something of self remains yet unsurrendered. Not until death is
swallowed up in victory, and perennial light overflows the uttermost bounds
of darkness, not until celestial glory clothes our bodies, can our souls be
freed entirely from self and give themselves up to God. For until then souls*

are bound to bodies, if not by a vital connection of sense, still by natural affection; so that without their bodies they cannot attain to their perfect consummation, nor would they if they could. And although there is no defect in the soul itself before the restoration of its body, since it has already attained to the highest state of which it is by itself capable, yet the spirit would not yearn for reunion with the flesh if without the flesh it could be consummated.

And finally, 'Right dear in the sight of the Lord is the death of His saints' (Ps. 116.15). But if their death is precious, what must such a life as theirs be! No wonder that the body shall seem to add fresh glory to the spirit; for though it is weak and mortal, it has availed not a little for mutual help. How truly he spake who said, 'All things work together for good to them that love God' (Rom. 8.28). The body is a help to the soul that loves God, even when it is ill, even when it is dead, and all the more when it is raised again from the dead: for illness is an aid to penitence; death is the gate of rest; and the resurrection will bring consummation. So, rightly, the soul would not be perfected without the body, since she recognizes that in every condition it has been needful to her good.

St. Bernard of
Clairvaux. *On Loving
God*, Ch. 11

Additional Biblical Reflections: John 6:40; 2 Corinthians 4:14; Romans 6:5.

Prayer

Lord, you have created us in body and soul and declared all things good. It is not the body, which is a gift given to us, that is to blame when we ail or when our bodies fail. It is, rather, the sin of this world that Christ has already defeated, along with the grave. Grant us confidence, likewise, to cherish our bodies in death so that we might see through the grave to our own glorification in Christ. Amen.

A MEDITATION FROM
ST. JOHN CASSIAN

Those who are sick, our Lord tells us, are as Christ to us. When we love the sick and the lowly, our Lord tells us, we love Him. When we serve those who are ailing, we are serving Jesus Himself. Thus, even the sick and dying are a great gift to those who are healthy and well. All of us will have the chance to take both the place of the healthy and sick. When we are healthy, let us love Christ by so loving the sick. When we are ill, let us humbly allow ourselves to stand in place of Christ for our fellows so that by loving us, they might draw closer to the heart of Christ.

A Meditation from St. John Cassian

After evening service we sat down together on the mats as usual ready for the promised narration: and when we had kept silence for some little time out of reverence for the Elder, he anticipated the silence of our respect by such words as these. The previous order of our discourse had brought us to the exposition of the system of spiritual gifts, which we have learned from the tradition of the Elders is a threefold one. The first indeed is for the sake of healing, when the grace of signs accompanies certain elect and righteous men on account of the merits of their holiness, as it is clear that the apostles and many of the saints wrought signs and wonders in accordance with the authority of the Lord Who says: Heal the sick, raise the dead, cleanse the lepers, cast out devils: freely you have received, freely give. The second when for the edification of the church or on account of the faith of those who bring their sick, or of those who are to be cured, the virtue of health proceeds even from sinners and men unworthy of it. Of whom the Saviour says in the gospel: Many shall say to Me in that day, Lord, Lord, have we not prophesied in Your name, and in Your name cast out devils, and in Your name done many mighty works? And then I will confess to them, I never knew you: Depart from Me, you workers of iniquity. And on the other hand, if the faith of those who bring them or of the sick is wanting, it prevents those on whom the gifts of healing are conferred from exercising their powers of healing. On which subject Luke the Evangelist says: And Jesus could not there do any mighty work because of their unbelief. Whence also the Lord Himself says: Many lepers were in Israel in the days of Elisha the prophet, and none of them was cleansed but Naaman the Syrian. The third method of healing is copied by the deceit and contrivance of devils, that, when a man who is enslaved to evident sins is out of admiration for his miracles regarded as a saint and a servant of God, men may be persuaded to copy his sins and thus an opening being made for caviling, the sanctity of religion may be brought into disgrace, or else that he, who believes that he possesses the gift of healing, may be puffed up by pride of heart and so fall more grievously. Hence it is that invoking the names of those, who, as they know, have no merits of holiness or any spiritual fruits, they pretend that by their merits they are disturbed and made to flee from the bodies they have possessed.

St. John Cassian, *The
Second Conference of
Abbot Nesteros*

Additional Biblical Reflections: Deuteronomy 13:1–3; Matthew 10:8; Mark 6:5–6; Luke 4:27.

Prayer

Lord, you have baptized us into your body. We are buried with you and therefore risen with you together as one body, the body of Christ, which you have also called your Church. Grant that we might both see Christ in one another and be Christ to our fellows so that we might live in your love through our love of one another. Amen.

A MEDITATION FROM ST. THERESE OF LISIEUX

s St. Therese of Lisieux fell ill, nearing death, even in her early twenties, she found a powerful metaphor to describe her condition: That of a little springtime white flower. A flower spends most of its life growing and blooms only shortly before it fails and dies. Likewise, the flower turns toward the sun so that it might receive its radiance. Similarly, as our bodies near death, we, too, must turn toward the Son and gladly receive His brilliance and glory.

A Meditation from St. Therese of Lisieux

I do not know how to describe this extraordinary illness. I said things which I had never thought of; I acted as though I were forced to act in spite of myself; I seemed nearly always to be delirious; and yet I feel certain that I was never, for a minute, deprived of my reason. Sometimes I remained in a state of extreme exhaustion for hours together, unable to make the least movement, and yet, in spite of this extraordinary torpor, hearing the least whisper. I remember it still. And what fears the devil inspired! I was afraid of everything; my bed seemed to be surrounded by frightful precipices; nails in the wall took the terrifying appearance of long fingers, shriveled and blackened with fire, making me cry out in terror. One day, while Papa stood looking at me in silence, the hat in his hand was suddenly transformed into some horrible shape, and I was so frightened that he went away sobbing.

But if God allowed the devil to approach me in this open way, Angels too were sent to console and strengthen me. Marie never left me, and never showed the least trace of weariness in spite of all the trouble I gave her—for I could not rest when she was away. During meals, when Victoire took care of me, I never ceased calling tearfully, "Marie! Marie!" When she wanted to go out, it was only if she were going to Mass or to see Pauline that I kept quiet. As for Léonie and my little Céline, they could not do enough for me. On Sundays they shut themselves up for hours with a poor child who seemed almost to have lost her reason. My own dear sisters, how much I made you suffer! My uncle and aunt were also devoted to me. My aunt came to see me every day, and brought me many little gifts. I could never tell you how my love for these dear ones increased during this illness. I understood better than ever what Papa had so often told us: "Always remember, children, that your uncle and aunt have devoted themselves to you in a way that is quite exceptional." In his old age he experienced this himself, and now he must bless and protect those who lavished on him such affectionate care. When my sufferings grew less, my great delight was to weave garlands of daisies and forget-me-nots for Our Lady's statue. We were in the beautiful month of May, when all nature is clothed with the flowers of spring; the Little Flower alone drooped, and seemed as though it had withered forever. Yet she too had a shining Sun, the miraculous statue of the Queen of Heaven. How often did not the Little Flower turn towards this glorious Sun!

St. Therese, *The Story of
the Springtime of a Little
White Flower*

Additional Biblical Reflections: Psalm 103:15–16; Matthew 6:25–34; Luke 12:22–32.

Prayer

Lord, death was never a part of your plan. When you hewed us from the dust, you intended for us to live in your glory forever. Nonetheless, despite our sin, you have redeemed even death itself so that as we draw near to it, we blossom the most, and our lives progress every more toward this glorious end where we, too, might join you in your death and endure until life eternal. Let us always turn toward the Son, especially when we are sick or near death so that we might embrace the glory that you have reserved for us. In Jesus' name. Amen.

A MEDITATION FROM
ST. GREGORY OF NYSSA

Creation itself testifies to the truth that death gives way to life. As the seasons change and the plants die in the fall and winter, the spring always births new life. Therefore, even the grasses of the field testify to the truth that death is but a season that gives way to the life of resurrection Spring.

A Meditation from St. Gregory of Nyssa

Having, then, all these considerations in our view, we hold that the soul of him who has reached every virtue in his course, and the soul of him whose portion of life has been simply nothing, are equally out of the reach of those sufferings which flow from wickedness. Nevertheless we do not conceive of the employment of their lives as on the same level at all. The one has heard those heavenly announcements, by which, in the words of the Prophet, the glory of God is declared, and, travelling through creation, has been led to the apprehension of a Master of the creation; he has taken the true Wisdom for his teacher, that Wisdom which the spectacle of the Universe suggests; and when he observed the beauty of this material sunlight he had grasped by analogy the beauty of the real sunlight; he saw in the solid firmness of this earth the unchangeableness of its Creator; when he perceived the immensity of the heavens he was led on the road towards the vast Infinity of that Power which encompasses the Universe; when he saw the rays of the

20

sun reaching from such sublimities even to ourselves he began to believe, by the means of such phenomena, that the activities of the Divine Intelligence did not fail to descend from the heights of Deity even to each one of us; for if a single luminary can occupy everything alike that lies beneath it with the force of light, and, more than that, can, while lending itself to all who can use it, still remain self-centred and undissipated, how much more shall the Creator of that luminary become all in all, as the Apostle speaks, and come into each with such a measure of Himself as each subject of His influence can receive! Nay, look only at an ear of grain, at the germinating of some plant, at a ripe bunch of grapes, at the beauty of early autumn, whether in fruit or flower, at the grass springing unbidden, at the mountain reaching up with its summit to the height of the ether, at the springs on its slopes bursting from those swelling breasts, and running in rivers through the glens, at the sea receiving those streams from every direction and yet remaining within its limits, with waves edged by the stretches of beach and never stepping beyond those fixed boundaries of continent: look at these and such-like sights, and how can the eye of reason fail to find in them all that our education for Realities requires? Has a man who looks at such spectacles procured for himself only a slight power for the enjoyment of those delights beyond? Not to speak of the studies which sharpen the mind towards moral excellence, geometry, I mean, and astronomy, and the knowledge of the truth that the science of numbers gives, and every method that furnishes a proof of the unknown and a conviction of the known, and, before all these, the philosophy contained in the inspired Writings, which affords a complete purification to those who educate themselves thereby in the mysteries of God.

St. Gregory of Nyssa,
On Infants' Early Deaths

Additional Biblical Reflections: Psalm 34:18; John 14:1; Revelation 21:4.

Prayer

Lord, you have written the truth of death and resurrection into Creation itself as a testimony that we, who are more valuable than grass and flowers, might likewise reflect death and resurrection and thereby glorify Christ through our death and rebirth. Console us with this hope so that as we and those we love die, this is not an end but a transition into the next season of life in you. Amen.

A MEDITATION FROM ST. JOHN CHRYSOSTOM

Often when we are in the midst of sickness and suffering, it is hard to see God's broader purpose. Nonetheless, we know from experience and the testimony of Scripture and the saints that even such troubles can draw us closer to you in faith, hope, and love.

A Meditation from St. John Chrysostom

Considering these things then let us imitate the patience of our fellow-servant: for his paralysis is sufficient to brace up our souls: for no one can be so supine and indolent after having observed the magnitude of that calamity as not to endure bravely all evils which may befall him, even if they are more intolerable than all that were ever known. For not only his soundness but also his sickness has become a cause of the greatest benefit to us: for his cure has stimulated the souls of the hearers to speak the praise of the Lord, and his sickness and infirmity has encouraged you to patience, and urged you to match his zeal; or rather it has exhibited to you the lovingkindness of God. For the actual deliverance of the man to such a malady, and the protracted duration of his infirmity is a sign of the greatest care for his welfare. For as a gold refiner having cast a piece of gold into the furnace suffers it to be proved by the fire until such time as he sees it has become purer: even so God permits the souls of men to be tested by troubles until they become pure and transparent and have reaped much profit from this process of sifting: wherefore this is the greatest species of benefit.

St. John Chrysostom,
Homily on the Paralytic

Additional Biblical Reflections: Psalm 147:3; Romans 8:28; Matthew 5:4.

Prayer

Lord, while we see only what is in front of us, you see all things, the big picture, of both past and future. Let us endure whatever sufferings we endure, and let us take courage likewise as we care for those who suffer among us so that through these things, our faith might be refined, and we might persist in a greater hope than before. Amen.

A MEDITATION FROM ST. AMBROSE

In the Creed, we confess our belief in the communion of the saints. Saint Ambrose, eulogizing the death of his friend, Satyrus, reflected that despite his loving brother's loss, on account of the mystical communion that we share in Christ's Church, we are even closer to those who have departed than we were in this life. We live together with all believers of all times when we share in the gifts that Christ has granted us, most especially in His Eucharist and the hearing of His life-giving Word.

A Meditation from St. Ambrose

For why should I weep for you, my most loving brother, who was thus torn from me that you might be the brother of all? For I have not lost but changed my intercourse with you; before we were inseparable in the body, now we are undivided in affection; for you remain with me, and ever will remain. And, indeed, while you were living with me, our country never tore you from me, nor did you yourself ever prefer our country to me; and now you have become surety for that other country, for I begin to be no stranger there where the better portion of myself already is. I was never wholly engrossed in myself, but the greater part of each of us was in the other, yet we were each of us in Christ, in Whom is the whole sum of all, and the portion of each severally. This grave is more pleasing to me than your natal soil, in which is the fruit not of nature but of grace, for in that body which now lies lifeless lies the better work of my life, since in this body, too, which I bear is the richer portion of yourself.

And would that, as memory and gratitude are devoted to you, so, too, whatever time I have still to breathe this air, I could breathe it into your life, and that half of my time might be struck off from me and be added to yours! For it had been just that for those, whose use of hereditary property was always undivided, the period of life should not have been divided, or at least that we, who always without difference shared everything in common during life, should not have a difference in our deaths.

St. Ambrose, *On the
Death of Satyrus*

Additional Biblical Reflections: Romans 12:4–12; 1 Corinthians 12:12–17; 1 Thessalonians 4:17–11.

Prayer

Lord, even as death cannot separate us from you, neither does death truly separate us from one another. Let us, who either mourn the death of our loved ones or face death ourselves, recognize that we are closer even in death than in life, for thereby we have a share in your body, the communion of saints. Amen.

A MEDITATION FROM POPE ST. JOHN PAUL II

I n today's meditation, Pope Saint John Paul II reminds us that in illness, we experience a "visit by God" and an opportunity to express love for one another. There is no other power or ideology on Earth that can allow us to perceive sickness and suffering in such a way. In Christ, however, sickness need not be purely evil but can be an occasion for righteousness.

A Meditation from Pope St. John Paul II

Illness, which in everyday experience is perceived as a frustration of the natural life force, for believers becomes an appeal to "read" the new, difficult situation in the perspective which is proper to faith. Outside of faith, moreover, how can we discover in the moment of trial the constructive contribution of pain? How can we give meaning and value to the anguish, unease, and physical and psychic ills accompanying our mortal condition? What justification can we find for the decline of old age and the final goal of death, which, in spite of all scientific and technological progress, inexorably remain?

Yes, only in Christ, the incarnate Word, Redeemer of mankind and victor over death, is it possible to find satisfactory answers to such fundamental questions.

In the light of Christ's death and resurrection illness no longer appears as an exclusively negative event; rather, it is seen as a "visit by God", an opportunity "to release love, in order to give birth to works of love towards neighbour, in order to transform the whole of human civilization into a civilization of love" (*Apostolic Letter Salvifici doloris, n. 30*).

The history of the Church and of Christian spirituality offers very broad testimony of this. Over the centuries shining pages have been written of heroism in suffering accepted and offered in union with Christ. And no less marvellous pages have been traced out through humble service to the poor and the sick, in whose tormented flesh the presence of the poor, crucified Christ has been recognized.

Pope St. John Paul II,
Word Day of the Sick
Homily, 1993

Additional Biblical Reflections: Psalm 103:1–5; James 5:14–16; 1 Peter 2:24.

Prayer

Lord, even illness is a visit by You on account of Christ's death and resurrection. Let us see your love in our illness so that we might find true spiritual health, which endures any ailment that might befall the body. In Jesus' name. Amen.

A MEDITATION FROM ST. THERESA OF ÀVILA

The mystic saint, Theresa of Àvila, fell seriously ill many times in her life. She had long seasons when she could hardly move. As a woman of God, who fervently desired to serve others in charity, she often found herself praying for health only that she might serve God better. However, in her illness, she found that God had granted her a season to serve differently.

A Meditation from St. Theresa of Àvila

O my God, how I longed for the health to serve You better, and this was the cause of all my undoing! When I saw myself so paralyzed and still so young, and how the physicians of the world had dealt with me, I decided to invoke those of heaven to heal me. For though I bore m y illness most joyfully, I still wanted to get well. But sometimes I reflected that I might regain my health and yet be lost, and that it would be better to stay as I was. But I away thought that I should serve God much better if I recovered. This is our mistake, never to resign ourselves absolutely to what the Lord does, though He knows best what suits us.

St. Theresa of Avila, *A Life*

Additional Biblical Reflections: Job 5:17–20; Psalm 147:2–4; Proverbs 16:24.

Prayer

Lord, whether in sickness or health, you have called us to serve you in love. Grant that no matter what befalls us, we might see the opportunities you have given us to serve you differently. In Jesus' name. Amen.

A MEDITATION FROM ST. ATHANASIUS

T he Lord came to us in weakness so that we might find his strength even in our mortal bodies—yes, even as our bodies near death. Saint Athanasius exhorts us in today's meditation to look to Christ as the example as we endure weakness and death in this world.

A Meditation from St. Athanasius

Why, now that the common Saviour of all has died on our behalf, we, the faithful in Christ, no longer die the death as before, agreeably to the warning of the law; for this condemnation has ceased; but, corruption ceasing and being put away by the grace of the Resurrection, henceforth we are only dissolved, agreeably to our bodies' mortal nature, at the time God has fixed for each, that we may be able to gain a better resurrection. For like the seeds which are cast into the earth, we do not perish by dissolution, but sown in the earth, shall rise again, death having been brought to nought by the grace of the Saviour. Hence it is that blessed Paul, who was made a surety of the Resurrection to all, says: This corruptible must put on incorruption, and this mortal must put on immortality; but when this corruptible shall have put on incorruption, and this mortal shall have put on immortality, then shall be brought to pass the saying that is written, Death is swallowed up in victory. O death where is your sting? O grave where is your victory? Why, then, one might say, if it were necessary for Him to yield up His body to death in the stead of all, did He not lay it aside as man privately, instead of going as far as even to be crucified? For it were more fitting for Him to have laid His body aside honourably, than ignominiously to endure a death like this. Now, see to it, I reply, whether such an objection be not merely human, whereas what the Saviour did is truly divine and for many reasons worthy of His Godhead. Firstly, because the death which befalls men comes to them agreeably to the weakness of their nature; for, unable to continue in one stay, they are dissolved with time. Hence, too, diseases befall them, and they fall sick and die. But the Lord is not weak, but is the Power of God and Word of God and Very Life. If, then, He had laid aside His body somewhere in private, and upon a bed, after the manner of men, it would have been thought that He also did this agreeably to the weakness of His nature, and because there was nothing in him more than in other men. But since He was, firstly, the Life and the Word of God, and it was necessary, secondly, for the death on behalf of all to be accomplished, for this cause, on the one hand, because He was life and power, the body gained strength in Him; while on the other, as death must needs come to pass, He did not Himself take, but received at others' hands; the occasion of perfecting His sacrifice. Since it was not fit, either, that the Lord should fall sick, who healed the diseases of others; nor again was it right for that body to lose its strength, in which He gives strength to the weaknesses of others also. Why, then, did He not prevent death, as He did sickness? Because it was for this that He had the body, and it was unfitting to prevent it, lest the Resurrection also should be hindered, while yet it was equally unfitting for sickness to precede His death, lest it should be thought weakness on the part of Him that was in the body. Did He not then hunger? Yes; He hungered, agreeably to the properties of His body. But He did not perish of hunger, because of the Lord that wore it. Hence, even if He died to ransom all, yet He saw not corruption. For [His body] rose again in perfect soundness, since the body belonged to none other, but to the very Life.

St. Athanasius, *De Incarnatione Verbi Dei*

Additional Biblical Reflections: John 11:25–26; 1 Corinthians 15:42–44; 2 Corinthians 4:17–18.

Prayer

Lord, your meekness is strength. Your cross is life. Let us see in the example of Christ a pattern to follow as we endure what is corruptible so that we might put on what is incorruptible.

A MEDITATION FROM ST. JUSTIN MARTYR

In today's meditation, Saint Justin encourages us to consider Christ, who healed people in the body, raised the dead in the body, and even died and rose himself, so that we recognize our resurrections will also be in the body. While we who die will dwell with God in Heaven, we also recognize that thereafter, he will raise us again in perfected bodies.

A Meditation from St. Justin Martyr

If He had no need of the flesh, why did He heal it? And what is most forcible of all, He raised the dead. Why? Was it not to show what the resurrection should be? How then did He raise the dead? Their souls or their bodies? Manifestly both. If the resurrection were only spiritual, it was requisite that He, in raising the dead, should show the body lying apart by itself, and the soul living apart by itself. But now He did not do so, but raised the body, confirming in it the promise of life. Why did He rise in the flesh in which He suffered, unless to show the resurrection of the flesh? And wishing to confirm this, when His disciples did not know whether to believe He had truly risen in the body, and were looking upon Him and doubting, He said to them, You have not yet faith, see that it is I, etc. and He let them handle Him, and showed them the prints of the nails in His hands. And when they were by every kind of proof persuaded that it was

Himself, and in the body, they asked Him to eat with them, that they might thus still more accurately ascertain that He had in verity risen bodily; and He ate honey-comb and fish. And when He had thus shown them that there is truly a resurrection of the flesh, wishing to show them this also, that it is not impossible for flesh to ascend into heaven (as He had said that our dwelling-place is in heaven), He was taken up into heaven while they beheld, as He was in the flesh. If, therefore, after all that has been said, any one demand demonstration of the resurrection, he is in no respect different from the Sadducees, since the resurrection of the flesh is the power of God, and, being above all reasoning, is established by faith, and seen in works.

St. Justin Martyr, *On
the Resurrection*

Additional Biblical Reflections: Luke 24:32; Acts 1:9; Romans 14:8.

Prayer

Lord, when you came to our world, you healed the sick and resurrected the body as a testimony so that we might see ourselves in those whom you healed and raised. Grant us a hope that persists beyond our firmament to the promise of new life in you. Amen.

A MEDITATION FROM ST. GREGORY THE GREAT

S aint Gregory the Great, in his rule for pastoral care, encouraged his ministers to exhort the sick to patience. However, this is not a virtue founded solely in the strength of the human will or a wish that things improve. Rather, it is a virtue bathed in the blood of Jesus' scourge, suffering, death, and resurrection.

A Meditation from St. Gregory the Great

The sick are to be admonished, to the end that they may keep the virtue of patience, to consider incessantly how great evils our Redeemer endured from those whom He had created; that He bore so many vile insults of reproach; that, while daily snatching the souls of captives from the hand of the old enemy, He took blows on the face from insulting men; that, while washing us with the water of salvation, He hid not His face from the spittings of the faithless; that, while delivering us by His advocacy from eternal punishments, He bore scourges in silence; that, while giving to us everlasting honours among the choirs of angels, He endured buffets; that, while saving us from the prickings of our sins, He refused not to submit His head to thorns; that, while inebriating us with eternal sweetness, He accepted in His thirst the bitterness of gall; that He Who for us adored the Father though equal to Him in Godhead, when adored in mockery held His peace: that, while preparing life for the dead, He Who was Himself the

36

life came even unto death. Why, then, is it thought hard that man should endure scourges from God for evil-doing, if God underwent so great evils for well-doing? Or who with sound understanding can be ungrateful for being himself smitten, when even He Who lived here without sin went not hence without a scourge?

St. Gregory the Great,
Pastoral Rule, Book III

Additional Biblical Reflections: Lamentations 3:25–26; Romans 15:5; Hebrews 10:36.

Prayer

Lord, you endured great suffering in the body for our sake. Grant that we might draw our patience in our own sickness and suffering from your example so that we might persist through it even as you once did for our sake. Amen.

A MEDITATION FROM
ST. ATHANASIUS

Even though our Lord died and rose, and he suffered in the body, his did not fall sick unto death, nor did his hunger and other sufferings cause his body to fail. Rather, as St. Athanasius shows us, Jesus died willingly. He laid down his life; it was not taken from him. Thus, we see more than an example in Jesus' suffering; we see a testimony to the fact that He is Lord over all sickness, suffering, and death.

A Meditation from St. Athanasius

Hence, too, diseases befall them, and they fall sick and die. But the Lord is not weak, but is the Power of God and Word of God and Very Life. If, then, He had laid aside His body somewhere in private, and upon a bed, after the manner of men, it would have been thought that He also did this agreeably to the weakness of His nature, and because there was nothing in him more than in other men. But since He was, firstly, the Life and the Word of God, and it was necessary, secondly, for the death on behalf of all to be accomplished, for this cause, on the one hand, because He was life and power, the body gained strength in Him; while on the other, as death must needs come to pass, He did not Himself take, but received at others' hands; the occasion of perfecting His sacrifice. Since it was not fit, either, that the Lord should fall sick, who healed the diseases of others; nor again was it right for that body to lose its strength, in which He gives strength to the weaknesses of others also. Why, then, did He not prevent death, as He did sickness? Because it was for this that He had the body, and it was unfitting to prevent it, lest the Resurrection also should be hindered, while yet it was equally unfitting for sickness to precede His death, lest it should be thought weakness on the part of Him that was in the body. Did He not then hunger? Yes; He hungered, agreeably to the properties of His body. But He did not perish of hunger, because of the Lord that wore it. Hence, even if He died to ransom all, yet He saw not corruption. For [His body] rose again in perfect soundness, since the body belonged to none other, but to the very Life.

St. Athanasius, *De Incarnatione Verbi Dei*

Additional Biblical Reflections: John 10:18; 1 Timothy 2:6; 1 John 3:16.

Prayer

Dear God, you are the Lord over all sufferings, illnesses, life, and death. In you, these things have no hold. Grant, likewise, that we, who are one with you, might be Lords over these things in You who allow us to die, not that our lives might be taken from us but that they might be preserved and held in your hands. Amen.

A MEDITATION FROM
ST. THERESE OF LISIEUX

Faith is a powerful thing. In today's meditation, Saint Therese of Lisieux reflects on her sickness and suffering, a condition from which she would not recover, and recognized that in Faith, she might receive it as God's will and persist in obedience by willingly accepting the chalice that he has granted her.

A Meditation from St. Therese of Lisieux

And I should not suffer any disappointment, for when we expect nothing but suffering, then the least joy is a surprise; and later on suffering itself becomes the greatest of all joys, when we seek it as a precious treasure. But I know I shall never recover from this sickness, and yet I am at peace. For years I have not belonged to myself, I have surrendered myself wholly to Jesus, and He is free to do with me whatsoever He pleases. He has spoken to me of exile, and has asked me if I would consent to drink of that chalice. At once I essayed to grasp it, but He, withdrawing His Hand, showed me that my consent was all He desired. O my God! from how much disquiet do we free ourselves by the vow of obedience! Happy is the simple religious. Her one guide being the will of her superiors, she is ever sure of following the right path, and has no fear of being mistaken, even when it seems that her superiors are making a mistake. But if she ceases to consult the unerring compass, then at once her soul goes astray in barren wastes, where the waters of grace quickly fail. Dear Mother, you are the compass Jesus has given me to direct me safely to the Eternal Shore. I find it most sweet to fix my eyes upon you, and then do the Will of my Lord. By allowing me to suffer these temptations against Faith, He has greatly increased the spirit of Faith, which makes me see Him living in your soul, and through you communicating His holy commands. I am well aware that you lighten the burden of obedience for me, but deep in my heart I feel that my attitude would not change, nor would my filial affection grow less, were you to treat me with severity: and this because I should still see the Will of God manifesting itself in another way for the greater good of my soul.

St. Therese, *The Story of
the Springtime of a Little
White Flower*

Additional Biblical Reflections: Psalm 27:13–14; John 16:20, 33; Romans 8:28.

Prayer

Lord, while we might not understand why you have given us whatever lot we suffer in life, grant that we might accept these things faithfully and remain fixed on you in faith so that your will might be manifest in our bodies, lives, and even in our passing from this life into the next. Amen.

A MEDITATION FROM ST. JOHN CHRYSOSTOM

In today's meditation, Saint John Chrysostom encourages a congregation in mourning. They have experienced a loss of one of their own and are grieving. It is not a lack of faith to mourn—even Jesus wept at Lazarus's death. Nonetheless, in Christ, our mourning should not turn to despair.

A Meditation from St. John Chrysostom

That you have sustained a severe blow, and that the weapon directed from above has been planted in a vital part all will readily admit, and none even of the most rigid moralists will deny it; but since they who are stricken with sorrow ought not to spend their whole time in mourning and tears, but to make good provision also for the healing of their wounds, lest, if they be neglected their tears should aggravate the wound, and the fire of their sorrow become inflamed, it is a good thing to listen to words of consolation, and restraining for a brief season at least the fountain of your tears to surrender yourself to those who endeavor to console you. On this account I abstained from troubling you when your sorrow was at its height, and the thunderbolt had only just fallen upon you; but having waited an interval and permitted you to take your fill of mourning, now that you are able to look out a little through the mist, and to open your ears to those who attempt to comfort you, I also would second the words of your handmaids by some contributions of my own. *For while the tempest is still severe, and a full gale of sorrow is blowing, he who exhorts another to desist from grief would only provoke him to increased lamentations and having incurred his hatred would add fuel to the flame by such speeches besides being regarded himself as an unkind and foolish person. But when the troubled water has begun to subside, and God has allayed the fury of the waves, then we may freely spread the sails of our discourse. For in a moderate storm skill may perhaps play its part; but when the onslaught of the wind is irresistible experience is of no avail. For these reasons I have hitherto held my peace, and even now have only just ventured to break silence because I have heard from your uncle that one may begin to take courage, as some of your more esteemed handmaids are now venturing to discourse at length upon these matters, women also outside your own household, who are your kinsfolk, or are otherwise qualified for this office. Now if you allow them to talk to you I have the greatest hope and confidence that you will not disdain my words but do your best to give them a calm and quiet hearing. Under any circumstances indeed the female sex is the more apt to be sensitive to suffering; but when in addition there is youth, and untimely widowhood, and inexperience in business, and a great crowd of cares, while the whole life previously has been nurtured in the midst of luxury, and cheerfulness and wealth, the evil is increased many fold, and if she who is subjected to it does not obtain help from on high even an accidental thought will be able to unhinge her. Now I hold this to be the foremost and greatest evidence of God's care concerning you; for that you have not been overwhelmed by grief, nor driven out of your natural condition of mind when such great troubles suddenly concurred to afflict you was not due to any human assistance but to the almighty hand the understanding of which there is no measure, the wisdom which is past finding out, the Father of mercies and the God of all comfort. For He Himself it is said has smitten us, and He will heal us; He will strike, and He will dress the wound and make us whole.*

St. John Chrysostom,
Letter to a Young Widow

Additional Biblical Reflections: Ecclesiastes 3:4; Hosea 6:2; 2 Corinthians 1:3.

Prayer

Lord, you mourned even as we mourn. Grant, however, that we might be granted confidence in you so our mourning might turn into joy and that we might celebrate even the loss of our loved ones in gratitude that you have received them in heavenly glory. Amen.

A MEDITATION FROM
ST. AMBROSE

Today's meditation from Saint Ambrose builds on the theme of yesterday's reflection: That our grief over death is temporary. Nonetheless, we should not be chastised for our sorrow. It is right to mourn over death, yet our grief should be coupled with patience so that we might not be overcome by it but know greater joys through it.

A Meditation from St. Ambrose

It is now our purpose to demonstrate that death ought not to cause too heavy grief, because nature itself rejects this. And so they say that there was a law among the Lycians, commanding that men who gave way to grief should be clothed in female apparel, inasmuch as they judged mourning to be soft and effeminate in a man. And it is inconsistent that those who ought to offer their breast to death for the faith, for religion, for their country, for righteous judgment, and the endeavour after virtue, should grieve too bitterly for that in the case of others which, if a fitting cause required, they would seek for themselves. For how can one help shrinking from that in ourselves which one mourns with too little patience when it has happened to others? Put aside your grief, if you can; if you cannot, keep it to yourself.

Is, then, all sorrow to be kept within or repressed? Why should not reason rather than time lighten one's sadness? Shall not wisdom better assuage that which the passage of time will obliterate? Further, it seems to me that it is a want of due feeling with regard to the memory of those whose loss we mourn, when we prefer to forget them rather than that our sorrow should be lessened by consolation; and to shrink from the recollection of them, rather than remember them with thankfulness; that we fear the calling to mind of those whose image in our hearts ought to be a delight; that we are rather distrustful than hopeful regarding the acceptance of the departed, and think of those we loved rather as liable to punishment than as heirs of immortality.

But you may say: We have lost those whom we used to love. Is not this the common lot of ourselves and the earth and elements, that we cannot keep forever what has been entrusted to us for a time? The earth groans under the plough, is lashed by rains, struck by tempests, bound by cold, burnt by the sun, that it may bring forth its yearly fruits; and when it has clothed itself with a variety of flowers, it is stripped and spoiled of its own adornment. How many plunderers it has! And it does not complain of the loss of its fruits, to which it gave birth that it might lose them, nor thereafter does it refuse to produce what it remembers will be taken from it.

The heavens themselves do not always shine with the globes of twinkling stars, wherewith as with coronets they are adorned. They are not always growing bright with the dawn of light, or ruddy with the rays of the sun; but in constant succession that most pleasing appearance of the world grows dark with the damp chill of night. What is more grateful than the light? What more pleasant than the sun? Each of which daily comes to an end; yet we do not take it ill that these have passed away from us, because we expect them to return. You are taught in these things what patience you ought to manifest with regard to those who belong to you. If things above pass away from you, and cause no grief, why should the passing away of man be mourned?

Let, then, grief be patient, let there be that moderation in adversity which is required in prosperity. If it be not seemly to rejoice immoderately, is it seemly so to mourn? For want of moderation in grief or fear of death is no small evil. How many has it driven to the halter, in how many hands has it placed the sword, that they might by that very means demonstrate their madness in not enduring death, and yet seeking it; in adopting that as a remedy which they flee from as an evil. And because they were unable to endure and to suffer what is in agreement with their nature, they fall into that which is contrary to their desire, being separated for ever from those whom they desired to follow. But this is not common, since nature herself restrains although madness drives men on.

St. Ambrose, *On the Death of Satyrus*

Additional Biblical Reflections: Psalm 18:2; Psalm 31:9; 1 Thessalonians 4:13.

Prayer

Lord, though we grieve, grant us patience. Thou we mourn, let us do so in moderation. Let us never wallow in darkness, but even in grief, see the light that breaks through and shines even more brightly in our sorrows. Amen.

A MEDITATION FROM POPE ST. JOHN PAUL II

In today's meditation, Pope St. John Paul II compares death to a gateway, a doorway, through which we pass. This gateway opens, solely for Christ's sake, to salvation and life. Nonetheless, this is a "required passage" through which we must pass to enter the fullness of immortal life. Likewise, in Baptism, we have a portion of Christ's design for our redemption and salvation from death to life.

A Meditation from Pope St. John Paul II

In the death and Resurrection of the Redeemer human suffering finds its deepest meaning and its saving value. All of the weight of humanity's affliction and pain is summarized in the mystery of a God who, taking on our human nature, was humiliated "for our sake... to be sin" (II Cor 5: 21). On Golgotha he was burdened with the sin of every human creature, and in solitude and abandonment he called out to the Father: "Why have you forsaken me?" (Mt 27: 46).

From the paradox of the Cross springs the answer to our most worrying questions. Christ suffers for us. He takes upon himself the sufferings of everyone and redeems them. Christ suffers with us, enabling us to share our pain with him. United to the suffering of Christ, human suffering becomes a means of salvation; this is why the believer can say with St Paul: "Now I rejoice in my sufferings for your sake, and in my flesh I complete what is lacking in Christ's afflictions for the sake of his body, that is, the Church." Pain, accepted with faith, becomes the doorway to the mystery of the Lord's redemptive suffering; a suffering that no longer takes away peace and happiness since it is illuminated by the splendour of the Resurrection.

At the foot of the Cross Mary, made Mother of humanity, suffers in silence, participating in her Son's suffering, ready to intercede so that every person may obtain salvation (cf. John Paul II, Apostolic Letter Salvifici Doloris [11 February 1984], n. 25; ORE, 20 February 1984, p. 6).

At Lourdes, it is not difficult to understand Mary's unique participation in the salvific role of Christ. The prodigy of the Immaculate Conception reminds believers of a fundamental truth: it is possible to reach salvation only through docile participation in the project of the Father, who wanted to redeem the world through the death and Resurrection of his only-begotten Son. Through Baptism, the believer becomes part of this design of salvation and is freed from original sin. Sickness and death, although present in earthly existence, lose their negative sense, and in the light of faith, corporal death, overcome by Christ's death, becomes the required passage for entering the fullness of immortal life.

Pope St. John Paul II,
Word Day of the Sick
Homily, 2004

Additional Biblical Reflections: Colossians 1:24; Romans 6:4; 2 Corinthians 5:21.

Prayer

Lord, death often stares at us like looming darkness. In you, however, it is but a doorway that opens up into the light of life everlasting. In faith, therefore, grant that we might face this required passage with confidence so that we might enter into your everlasting glory. In Jesus' name. Amen.

9 781667 304267